a Bride

WITHOUT SPOT *or* WRINKLE

Thelma C. Smith

CREATION HOUSE
A STRANG COMPANY

A Bride Without Spot or Wrinkle
by Thelma C. Smith
Published by Creation House
A Strang Company
600 Rinehart Road
Lake Mary, Florida 32746
www.strangbookgroup.com

Unless otherwise noted, all Scripture quotations are from the New King James Version of the Bible. Copyright © 1979, 1980, 1982 by Thomas Nelson, Inc., publishers. Used by permission.

Scripture quotations marked KJV are from the King James Version of the Bible.

Scripture quotations marked NIV are from the Holy Bible, New International Version of the Bible. Copyright © 1973, 1978, 1984, International Bible Society. Used by permission.

Scripture quotations marked NLT are from the Holy
Bible, New Living Translation, copyright © 1996.
Used by permission of Tyndale House Publishers, Inc.,
Wheaton, IL 60189. All rights reserved.

Design Director: Bill Johnson

Cover design by Rachel Lopez

Library of Congress Control Number: 2010931339
International Standard Book Number:
978-1-61638-199-8

First Edition

10 11 12 13 14 — 9 8 7 6 5 4 3 2 1
Printed in the United States of America

Contents

Acknowledgments

MANY THANKS...

- To my Lord and Savior Jesus Christ for giving me the inspiration to write this book.

- To my husband, Pierce, for his patience, love, and support.

- To my mom, Mildred Cromartie, for her unending love and support.

- To my daughter, Dawn, Dr. Sharon Byrd, Rev. Davine Brayboy, Doreen Stafford, and others who have given me editing assistance, prayer, and support.

- To the many who have helped me birth this book through prayer.

- To Virginia Maxwell, my editor at Creation House for the many hours of diligent labor and expertise in helping to complete this book.

Introduction

I INVITE YOU TO pray with me about an issue as old as Adam and Eve. In fact the issue began with the fall of man. I invite you to pray with me about the preparation of the bride of Christ for His return.

This book is different from many that you may read in its perspective and position. In the pages of this book you will see the parallels between the natural and the spiritual. It is written from a spiritual perspective that is not often publicly acknowledged, even though it is based entirely on the Bible, the inerrant Word of God. The bride referred to in this book, as well as in the Scripture, is the church, the body of believers in Christ worldwide. Comparison is made in the Scripture between a natural bride and the church to give us understanding of an important spiritual concept. Things in the natural are often reflective of things in the spirit. For example, the church is often referred to as Israel or Jerusalem or Zion (Psalm 87; Luke 1:33; 1 Peter 2:4–10). Many religious leaders will say, as the country of Israel and its holy city Jerusalem goes, so goes the church. That is why it is imperative that we continue to pray for and support Israel. Israel's becoming a country again in 1948 is something that was prophesied in Scripture. We must encourage Israel to not give up any of its land. Its land is a divine land grant given by God which is described in Genesis 15:18. The church has given up too much of its place in the world. We are mandated to be salt and light in the Earth, not just within the walls of our church or with our own congregations. We are to have dominion in the Earth, and our influence should bring blessings to anywhere we inhabit, work, or travel. Christ is returning for a bride without spot or wrinkle. I invite you to pray with me for the bride of Christ and the deliverance of women worldwide. The plight of women in this world is reflective of the church. In the scripture below from Ephesians, the mystery that is spoken of makes clear how the relationship between Christ and the church is reflective of the relationship between a man and his wife.

> Husbands, love your wives, just as Christ also loved the church and gave Himself for her, that He might sanctify and cleanse her with the

washing of water by the word, that He might present her to Himself a glorious church, not having spot or wrinkle or any such thing, but that she should be holy and without blemish. So husbands ought to love their own wives as their own bodies; he who loves his wife loves himself. For no one ever hated his own flesh, but nourishes and cherishes it, just as the Lord does the church. For we are members of His body, of His flesh and of His bones. *"For this reason a man shall leave his father and mother and be joined to his wife, and the two shall become one flesh."* This is a great mystery, but I speak concerning Christ and the church. Nevertheless let each one of you in particular so love his own wife as himself, and let the wife see that she respects her husband.
—Ephesians 5:25–33, emphasis added

This book and prayer ministry will bring revelation to how the relationship between men and women affects the body of Christ, His bride, on a global scale.

The intent of this work is to focus prayer in spiritual realms to bring deliverance to women and restoration and transformation to the body of Christ. Prayer in the name of Jesus is a spiritual weapon that is able to tear down all spiritual strongholds. These strongholds may be thought patterns or logic. They may be anything that exalts itself against the knowledge of God. Strongholds may be ideologies, temptations, plans, or devices that do not line up with the Word of God. Second Corinthians 10:3–5 (NLT) states:

> We are human, but we don't wage war with human plans and methods. We use God's mighty weapons, not mere worldly weapons, to knock down the Devil's strongholds. With these weapons we break down every proud argument that keeps people from knowing God. With these weapons we conquer their rebellious ideas, and we teach them to obey Christ.

I invite you to pray with me about the preparation of the bride of Christ for His return.

chapter 1
Why We Pray

*I*T IS SO important to pray the will of God in the Earth—to speak it forth by faith in prayer. This is how we war in the spirit and tear down spiritual strongholds.

> For the weapons of our warfare are not carnal but mighty in God to the pulling down strongholds.
> —2 CORINTHIANS 10:3–4

> You shall declare a thing and it shall be established for you; so will light shine on your ways.
> —JOB 22:28

> Now this is the confidence that we have in Him, that if we ask anything according to His will, He hears us. And if we know that He hears us, whatever we ask, we know that

we have the petitions that we have asked of Him.

—1 John 5:14–15

For the word of God is living and powerful, and sharper than any two-edged sword, piercing even to the division of soul and spirit, and of joints and marrow, and is a discerner of the thoughts and intents of the heart.

—Hebrews 4:12

He had in His right hand seven stars, out of His mouth went a sharp two-edged sword, and His countenance was like the sun shining in its strength.

—Revelation 1:16

As we speak what God speaks in agreement with His Word, it becomes a great spiritual weapon.

So shall My word be that goes forth from My mouth; It shall not return to Me void, But it shall accomplish what I please, And it shall prosper in the thing for which I sent it.

—Isaiah 55:11

This understanding of God's Word in prayer; this understanding of what Christ has accomplished for us on the cross; this understanding of God's will in the Earth; the anointing that He put in us and the authority that He has given us are the keys to the kingdom.

> And I will give you the keys of the kingdom of heaven, and whatever you bind on earth will be bound in heaven, and whatever you loose on earth will be loosed in heaven.
> —Matthew 16:19

These keys have great spiritual significance. This means that spiritual forces that once held us in bondage will be broken, literally at our word. Spiritual forces that come against us to harm us will be bound at our word, as we pray. Christ has given us the victory! He openly put the enemy to shame. The enemy is a defeated foe. We want women everywhere to know this and begin to walk in the freedom that is theirs in Jesus Christ, our marvelous, wonderful Savior.

> Stand fast therefore in the liberty by which Christ has made us free.
> —Galatians 5:1

Therefore if the Son makes you free, you shall
be free indeed.

—JOHN 8:36

Press on toward the prize of the high calling of
God to fulfill His will in the earth.

I see the church triumphant and victorious, the
bride without spot or wrinkle, ready for Jesus' return.

chapter 2

Co-dominion: What the Enemy Does Not Want Women to Know

The church and the world are in a place poised for Jesus' return. The whole earth groans and "eagerly waits for the revealing of the sons of God" (Rom. 8:19). We contend for the manifestation of the sons of God to be revealed. God, teach our hands to war in the spirit so that our prayers will be powerful and far reaching like an arrow shot from a "bow of bronze" (Ps. 18:34). We pray that God's presence and power move among individuals, families, and the nations. From this time onward, I pray that lives will forever be changed, as they begin to move into the places that You have prepared for them, that Your return would hasten, for

*Your Word does not return void. We thank
You, Father, in Jesus' name, Amen.*

𝒥N THIS HOUR of restoration, God is moving
in His church to prepare us to receive and
walk in all that He has promised. As we look at this
present time with all of the wickedness and trouble
in the world, God is expecting His church through
the power of Christ to multiply, to subdue the Earth,
and to take dominion.

> For the earnest expectation of the creation
> eagerly waits for the revealing of the sons of
> God.
>
> —ROMANS 8:19

God truly desires to do a miraculous transformation in us that is "exceedingly abundantly above
all that we ask or think" (Eph. 3:20). Psalm 102:13
(KJV) declares:

> Thou shalt arise, and have mercy upon Zion:
> for the time to favour her, yea, the set time,
> is come.

We Must Realize
Who We Are in Christ

If God's purpose is going to be realized in and through the bride, we must come to realize who we are in Christ. The Word of the Lord in Ephesians 2:6 declares:

> [He has] raised us up together, and made us sit together in the heavenly places in Christ Jesus....

In this day of restoration of the church, God is making it clear that both men and *women* must take their rightful places in the kingdom—the husband and the *wife*, walking in biblical knowledge of created purpose, walking in *co-dominion* in the Earth as the Word clearly declares:

> So God created man in His own image; in the image of God He created him; male and female He created them. Then God blessed them, and God said to them, "Be fruitful and multiply; fill the earth and subdue it; have dominion over the fish of the sea, over the birds of the air, and over every living thing that moves on the earth."
> —Genesis 1:27–28

When God created the heavens and the Earth, the relationship between a man and a woman was not as it is today. There was co-dominion in the garden before the fall. There was a curse placed on Adam and Eve because of their sin. When Jesus came to set us free from the curses, men began to walk in their freedom, but women have been expected to remain under the curse.

Genesis 3:15–16 describes the curse placed on women:

> "And I will put enmity Between you and the woman, And between your seed and her Seed; He shall bruise your head, and you shall bruise His heel." To the woman He said: "I will greatly multiply your sorrow and your conception; In pain you shall bring forth children; Your desire shall be for your husband, And he shall rule over you."

"He [the husband] shall rule over you" is part of the curse.

Before the fall, if you look at Genesis 1:27, male and female were to "Be fruitful and multiply; to fill the earth and subdue it; have dominion...." There was *co-dominion* of the earth by male and female.

In the family, man was created first and is to be head of the family. But, in the Earth, there was co-dominion by male and female. When we stand before God, we are joint heirs, as it was in the beginning, because of the power that is in the precious blood of Jesus.

Ephesians 5:22–33 describes the parallel relationships of husbands and wives and Christ and the church. The Bible is written in symbols, types, and parables to give us earthly symbols that we recognize to help give us understanding of spiritual realities that would otherwise be beyond our comprehension. The scripture that tells us "wives are to submit to their own husbands in love," was designed to bring order in the home. This relationship is not to diminish the capabilities of a woman's mind or her sovereign or creative authority, but as a joint heir, she becomes a mighty force exercising kingdom authority in the earth.

If you look at Proverbs 31, the wife described here was an entrepreneur, a prosperous businesswoman and landowner, who ran the affairs of her household, but also the affairs of her business. She blessed those in need in her community, her children and household, and her husband in all that she did.

She goes to inspect a field and buys it; with her earnings she plants a vineyard. She is energetic and strong, a hard worker. She makes sure her dealings are profitable; her lamp burns late into the night....She extends a helping hand to the poor and opens her arms to the needy. She has no fear of winter for her household, for everyone has warm clothes. She makes her own bedspreads. She dresses in fine linen and purple gowns. Her husband is well known at the city gates, where he sits with the other civic leaders. She makes belted linen garments and sashes to sell to the merchants.

—PROVERBS 31:16–18, 20–24, NLT

In the New Testament, Paul makes clear the position of all in Christ.

There is neither Jew nor Greek, there is neither slave nor free, there is neither male nor female; for you are all one in Christ Jesus. And if you *are* Christ's, then you are Abraham's seed, and heirs according to the promise.

—GALATIANS 3:28–29

God's thoughts of women are not that they are less than or beneath, or to be controlled and manipulated. They are to be loved, protected, and cherished according to His Word.

God has always acknowledged women in ministry. Consider the following examples!

- Miriam the prophetess, the sister of Aaron (Exod. 15:20)

- Huldah the prophetess, the wife of Shallum (2 Kings 22:14)

- Deborah, a prophetess, the wife of Lapidoth, was judging Israel at that time (Judges 4:4).

- Anna, a prophetess, daughter of Phanuel, announced that salvation had come through Jesus (Luke 2:36).

- Mary Magdalene was the first to announce Jesus' resurrection (John 20:14–18):

Now when she had said this, she turned around and saw Jesus standing there, and did not know that it was Jesus. Jesus said to her, "Woman, why are you weeping? Whom are you seeking?" She, supposing Him to be the gardener, said to Him, "Sir, if You have carried Him away, tell me where You have laid Him, and I will take Him away." Jesus said to her, "Mary!" She turned and said to Him, "Rabboni!" (which is to say, Teacher)....but go to My brethren and say to them, "I am ascending to My Father and your Father, and to My God and your God." Mary Magdalene came and told the disciples that she had seen the Lord, and that He had spoken these things to her.

- In the Upper Room

And when they had entered, they went up into the upper room where they were staying: Peter, James, John, and Andrew; Philip and Thomas; Bartholomew and Matthew; James the son of Alphaeus and Simon the Zealot; and Judas the son of James. These all continued with one accord in prayer and supplication, with *the women and Mary the mother of Jesus,* and with His brothers. And in those days Peter stood up in the midst of the disciples (altogether the number of names was about a hundred and twenty).

—ACTS 1:1–15, EMPHASIS ADDED

- On the Day of Pentecost

But this is what was spoken by the prophet Joel: 'And it shall come to pass in the last days, says God, That I will pour out of My Spirit on all flesh; Your sons and your *daughters* shall prophesy, Your young men shall see visions, Your old men shall dream dreams. And on My menservants and on My *maidservants* I will pour out My Spirit in those days; *And they shall prophesy.*

—ACTS 2:16–18, EMPHASIS ADDED

- Philip's daughters

Philip the evangelist, who was one of the seven, and stayed with him. Now this man had four virgin daughters who prophesied.

—ACTS 21:8–9

- Paul commends many women who labored in the faith with him (Rom. 16): Junia (the first female apostle), Priscilla, Phoebe, Mary, Julia, Tryphaena, and Tryphosa

In the same way, you husbands must give honor to your wives. Treat her with understanding as

> you live together. She may be weaker than you
> are, but *she is your equal partner in God's gift of*
> *new life.* If you don't treat her as you should,
> your prayers will not be heard.
> —1 PETER 3, EMPHASIS ADDED

Women must know and understand what God says about them so that their thinking aligns with His plan. How we think will determine our behavior. The enemy cannot defeat us if he cannot control our thoughts. Our minds must be renewed by the Word of God. Our hearts must be conformed to His will. We must be willing to go through the process of cleansing and pruning so that we can grow to become all that God intended and produce the fruit that He requires.

The enemy desires to keep women under a curse. Jesus shed His blood to set women and men free from all curses. God desires to prepare women to receive all the promises of His Word.

Because there is enmity between the devil and women, the devil does not want them to realize who they are in Christ. God has provided the way for women to assume their rightful position in the kingdom in co-dominion, in a place of trust, not in competition.

chapter 3
Prayer Targets

BEFORE WE ENTREAT the Lord, it is important that we enter into His gates with thanksgiving and into His court with praise. Then He will bring us into His presence in worship. "They overcame him with the blood of the Lamb and the word of their testimony" (Rev 12:11). When we tell others and thank God for what He has done for us, it is a method to overcome the enemy. Thanksgiving, praise, and worship are spiritual weapons, and through them we enter into the presence of God. First thanksgiving, then praise, and finally worship is the correct pattern to enter into God's presence. This is a pattern that is established in Scripture in Psalm 100:4 and throughout the description of the temple of God. There are the outer courts, the inner court, and the holy of holies, signifying thanksgiving, praise, and worship as the pattern. When we are in God's presence, He transforms us to become more like His Son. He takes us "from glory to glory"

(2 Cor. 3:18). One can use Scripture made personal in the giving of thanks and praise, or one can use his or her own personal experience. However you enter in, your access is granted through your thanksgiving and praise. As you seek the Lord, speak out loud to Him your thanksgiving, praise, and worship as you pray. When you do so, the Lord will create the atmosphere for your healing and deliverance. The spoken word has creative power!

> You will also declare a thing, And it will be established for you: So light will shine on your ways.
>
> —JOB 22:28

> So shall My word be that goes forth from My mouth; It shall not return to Me void, But it shall accomplish what I please, And it shall prosper in the thing for which I sent it.
>
> —ISAIAH 55:11

The Scripture says, "For the word of God is alive and powerful. It is sharper than the sharpest two-edged sword, cutting between soul and spirit, between joint and marrow. It exposes our innermost thoughts and desires" (Heb. 4:12, NLT). God wants to heal the hidden places. The Word has been given, and it is sufficient to address every area of our lives. When we apply the Word to ourselves, we activate the power of the Word into our circumstances and our lives. An example is taken from Psalm 107:

> [I] give thanks to the LORD, for He is good!
> For His mercy endures forever.
> [I am] the redeemed of the LORD [and I say so],
> Whom He has redeemed from the hand of
>   the enemy,
> And gathered out of the lands,
> From the east and from the west,
> From the north and from the south.
>
> [I] wandered in the [spiritual] wilderness in a
>   desolate way;
> [I] found no city to dwell in.
> Hungry and thirsty,
> [My] soul fainted in [me].
> Then [I] cried out to the LORD in [my] trouble,
> And He delivered [me] out of [my] distresses.
> And He led [me] forth by the right way,
> That [I] might go to a city for a dwelling place.
> Oh, [I] give thanks to the LORD for His
>   goodness,

And for His wonderful works to the children
    of men!
For He satisfies [my] longing soul,
And fills the hungry soul with goodness.

[I] sat in darkness and in the shadow of death,
Bound in affliction and irons [from my sins]—
Because [I] rebelled against the words of God,
And despised the counsel of the Most High,
Therefore He brought down[my] heart with
    labor;
[I] fell down, and there was none to help.
Then [I] cried out to the LORD in [my] trouble,
And He saved me out of [my] distresses.
He brought [me] out of darkness and the
    shadow of death,
And broke [my] chains in pieces.
Oh, [I] give thanks to the LORD for His
    goodness,
And for His wonderful works to the children
    of men!
For He has broken the gates of bronze,
And cut the bars of iron in two.

[I am a] fool, because of [my] transgression,
And because of my iniquities, [I] was afflicted.
[My] soul abhorred all manner of food,
And [I] drew near to the gates of death.

Then [I] cried out to the LORD in [my] trouble,
And He saved [me] out of [my] distresses.
He sent His word and healed [me],
And delivered [me] from [my] destructions.
Oh, [I] give thanks to the LORD for His
    goodness,
And for His wonderful works to the children
    of men!
[I] will sacrifice the sacrifices of thanksgiving,
And declare His works with rejoicing.

[I] who go down to the sea in ships,
[I] do business on great waters,
[I] see the works of the LORD,
And His wonders in the deep.
For He commands and raises the stormy wind,
Which lifts up the waves of the sea.
They mount up to the heavens,
They go down again to the depths;
[My] soul melts because of trouble.
[I] reel to and fro, and stagger like a
    drunken [person],
And am at [my] wits' end.
Then [I] cry out to the LORD in [my] trouble,
And He brings [me] out of [my] distresses.
He calms the storm,
So that its waves are still.

Then [I] am glad because they are quiet;
So He guides [me] to [my] desired haven.
Oh, [I] give thanks to the LORD for His
    goodness,
And for His wonderful works to the children
    of men!
[I] exalt Him also in the assembly of the
    people,
And praise Him in the company of the elders.

He turns rivers into a wilderness,
And the watersprings into dry ground;
A fruitful land into barrenness,
For [my] wickedness....
He turns a wilderness into pools of water,
And dry land into watersprings.
There He makes [me] dwell,
That [I] may establish a city for a dwelling
    place,
And sow fields and plant vineyards,
That [I] may yield a fruitful harvest.
He also blesses [me], and [I] multiply greatly;
And He does not let [my] cattle decrease.

When [I] am diminished and brought low
Through oppression, affliction and sorrow,
He pours contempt on princes,

And causes them to wander in the wilderness
    where there is no way;
Yet He sets [me] the poor on high, far from
    affliction,
And makes [my] family like a flock.
The righteous see it and rejoice,
And all iniquity stops its mouth.

Whoever is wise will observe these things,
And they will understand the lovingkindness
    of the LORD.

God has made provision for the church through Jesus' shed blood. We have authority over the enemy and no longer have to live in bondage and defeat. Unfortunately, there are billions of people on this planet who need Christ's salvation and deliverance. I entreat you to join with me in prayer for these. Throughout this chapter, I will address the curses described in Genesis 3:15–16 and share statistics from the United States and the world that relate to these Scriptures. These areas give us specific prayer targets where we can take dominion in prayer. Please join me in this endeavor. As blood-bought warriors, we have been given the privilege and honor to partner with Christ, to go into war in the Spirit and set the captives free.

"And I will put enmity between you and the woman, And between your seed and her Seed; He shall bruise your head, and you shall bruise His heel." To the woman He said: "I will greatly multiply your sorrow and your conception; In pain you shall bring forth children; Your desire shall be for your husband, And he shall rule over you."

—Genesis 3:15–16

The enemy hates women. He often uses men to accomplish his purposes! Some men blame women for the fall and therefore hate women. Women also believe the lie and, therefore, take the abuse.

A husband is called in the Word to love, cherish, and protect his wife. The LORD uses His relationship with the church as a metaphor for earthly covenant marriage:

Husbands, love your wives, just as Christ also loved the church and gave Himself for her.

—Ephesians 5:25

Statistical Evidence

- The number one cause of death among pregnant women is battering by a spouse or boyfriend;[1]

- 1 in 4 pregnant women are abused during pregnancy;[2]

- One third of all murders in the U.S. are women caused by a former spouse or boyfriend;[3]

- Each year more than 3,000 women are murdered in the U.S. by a former spouse or boyfriend;[4]

- 3–4 million women are assaulted by a male partner in the U.S. each year;[5]

- 1 in 3 women has been abused at some point in her life;[6]

- 40 percent of assaults on women by their male partners begin during the first pregnancy;[7]

- Pregnant women are at twice the risk of battery;[8]

- In some Muslim cultures, it is lawful for a man to beat his wife as long as he does not break any bones. Girls and women are not allowed to attend school, own businesses, or property.[9]

The data on divorce in America is high because we fail to realize our positions as joint heirs in Christ and we do not see ourselves as Abraham's seed, the seed of promise and of faith. Both male and female are seated in heavenly places. If by the power of God, men and women moved into their predestined purposes as joint rulers of God's kingdom, the data would reverse to reflect the image of Christ and his bride as God intended.

Consider the following data:

- Fifty percent of first marriages, 67 percent of second, and 74 percent of third marriages end in divorce.[10]

- Only 63 percent of American children grow up with both biological parents—the lowest figure in the Western world.[11]

- As of 2003, 43.7 percent of custodial
  mothers and 56.2 percent of custodial
  fathers were either separated or
  divorced. And in 2002, 7.8 million
  Americans paid about $40 billion
  in child and/or spousal support (84
  percent of the payers were male).[12]

The Word of God tells us that a three-fold cord
is not easily broken. Marriage is a three-fold cord
because a Christian marriage is a covenant between
the husband, the wife, and the Lord. When we leave
God and His power out of the equation, we open the
door for disaster to come.

PRAYER

Father, thank You that Your Word is true.
"Your truth endures to all generations."
Your "Word shall not return void." We come
to You in the precious name of Jesus. The
curse is broken because of the shed blood of
Jesus, and with it the enemy's power to kill
and destroy. Enmity is defined as opposi-
tion against an enemy. We bind the spirit of

murder and oppression. We loose this spirit from its assignment against women all over the planet. We declare that this enmity or opposition to women is destroyed through the shed blood of Jesus. Husbands will "love their own wives as their own bodies; he who loves his wife loves himself. For no one ever hated his own flesh, but nourishes and cherishes it, just as the Lord does the church."

Dispatch Your "angels who excel in strength" to guard, protect, and defend women every-where on this planet. Through the blood of Jesus we break the curse of anger, abuse, and opposition that is directed toward women and the church. By your Spirit, touch the hearts and minds of men and women. Draw them to You. Transform them by Your Spirit in the inner man. Restore broken marriages. Heal broken families. Thank You for Your love and protection where we can "walk through the valley of the shadow of death and fear no evil," where we can "abide in the shadow of the Almighty." "You are our fortress, our refuge, and our God in whom we trust." We release love, joy, peace, forgiveness, and mercy.

(Ps. 100:5; Gal. 3:13; Matt. 16:19; Eph. 5:28–29; Ps. 103:20; Rom. 12:1; Ps. 23:4; Ps. 91:1–2)

"...AND BETWEEN YOUR SEED AND HER SEED" (GEN. 3:15)

Women bring life into the world. The birth of Christ came through a woman to destroy the power of the enemy. Because of this great enmity between the devil and women's seed, there are huge numbers of deaths in the birthing process. Millions more are slaughtered in the abortion process. In China, girl babies are aborted because the families can only have one child, and the male is considered more valuable.

> Then the dragon was enraged at the woman and went off to make war against the rest of her offspring—those who obey God's commandments and hold to the testimony of Jesus.
>
> —REVELATION 12:17, NIV

What is happening in this world in the natural is the result of spiritual battles. Consider the following mortality statistics:[13]

- Of the estimated total of 536,000 maternal deaths worldwide in 2005, developing countries accounted for 99 percent (533,000) of these deaths.

- More than half of the maternal deaths (270,000) occurred in the sub-Saharan Africa region alone, followed by South Asia (188,000).

- Thus, sub-Saharan Africa and South Asia accounted for 86 percent of global maternal deaths.

Abortion statistics

- Worldwide, there are 115,000 abortions every day, which equals 42 million abortions per year.

- In the United States, there are 3,700 abortions every day, which equals 1.37 million per year.

- 45 million babies have been murdered in the U.S. since abortion was legalized.

- 93 percent of all abortions are done as a means of birth control.

- 1 percent are done because of rape or incest.

- 6 percent are done because of fetal abnormalities or because of the mother's health problems.[14]

There were 4.6 million births and 1.37 million abortions in America in 2006. More than one quarter of the population was willfully killed by abortion.

Human trafficking

Human trafficking is the second largest and fastest growing criminal industry in the world after arms and drug dealing. Traffickers prey on women and children for profit and gain.

- Over 12 million people worldwide are trafficked for forced labor or sexual exploitation.[15]

- Over 200,000 children are at high risk for sex trafficking and commercial sexual exploitation in the U. S. every year.[16]

The pornographic industry has larger revenue than all other technological industries combined.

PRAYER

Lord, "turn the hearts of the fathers to the children" to stop the curse. We plead the blood of Jesus and break the curse on the "abominable hands that shed innocent blood" and "hearts that devise wicked plans," against those that "sacrifice their sons and daughters to idols," against those "who lie in wait to shed the blood of the innocent without a cause," against those "who take a bribe to slay the innocent." God, forgive our nation for the horrible atrocities we have committed; for turning away from You and chasing prosperity, power, and convenience; for allowing prayer to be taken from schools and Your laws to be banished from public places; for the rampant sins and oppressions in our land and for what we have forced on other countries. Forgive us for our lewdness, perverseness, and immorality. God, forgive our sins. Have mercy. Turn us toward You, cleanse our hearts, and "renew a right spirit within" us. We bind the spirit of murder and immorality. We loose this spirit from its assignment against women and their seed on this planet, in the name of Jesus. By Jesus' blood the curse is broken. Restore our love for You, Your laws, and our children. Cleanse us and fill us with your Spirit, in Jesus' name, Amen.

(Mal. 4:6; Prov. 6:17–18; Ps. 106:37–38; Prov. 1:11; Deut. 25:27, 12:31; Ps. 51:10)

"HE SHALL BRUISE YOUR HEAD, AND YOU SHALL BRUISE HIS HEEL" (GEN. 3:15)

There are approximately 101 million born-again Christians in the U.S.[17] and about 800 million Christians in the world.[18] Through the death, burial, and resurrection of Jesus, the Messiah, we have victory! Yes, victory for every believer, past, present, and future rests in Christ Jesus; Jesus the Lamb of God born of a woman; Jesus, the power of God unto salvation, our deliver, healer, and advocate! Hear the Word of the Lord:

> And the God of peace will crush Satan under your feet shortly. The grace of our Lord Jesus Christ be with you.
> —ROMANS 16:20

> Now when the dragon saw that he had been cast to the earth, he persecuted the woman who gave birth to the male Child....And the dragon was enraged with the woman, and he went to make war with the rest of her offspring, who keep the commandments of God and have the testimony of Jesus Christ.
> —REVELATION 12:13, 17

PRAYER

Father, we thank You for the victory that You have provided for us through Your Son Jesus Christ. "He has openly put to shame and defeated the enemy." "One can chase a thousand; two can chase ten thousand." Father, I pray that the 800 million saints of God would come together as a mighty army in prayer and take back all that was taken from us. "The kingdom of heaven suffers violence, and the violent take it by force." We take back every area and destroy the works of the devil in the Earth and in the minds and hearts of men and women and children, in Jesus' name, for God has given us "authority over all the power of the enemy." We thank You for Your Holy Spirit that has been released in the Earth, for "it is not by might, nor by power, but by Your Spirit." "We wrestle not against flesh and blood, but against principalities, against powers, against the rulers of darkness of this world, against spiritual wickedness in high places." "We cast down every thought that is not in obedience to Christ." We thank You, Father, for the victory, in Jesus' name. Amen.

(Col. 2:15; Deut. 32:30, Matt. 11:12; Luke 10:19; Zech. 4:6; Eph. 6:12; 2 Cor. 10:5)

"I will greatly multiply your sorrow and your conception" (Gen. 3:16)

The world began with Adam and Eve. The blessing of fruitfulness was a gift to us from God. There were

4.6 million births in America in 2006, while there are 309 million Americans (2000 Census). There are 6.8 billion people on this planet.

In China, women over thirty-five are laid off from their jobs, because the younger women are considered more attractive and bring more business. In many cultures, women who never married and widows are not taken care of because there are no provisions in their system for their care. If a relative does not take them in, they usually end up as vagrants on the streets. Often, they are mistreated and abused, forgotten and lost. In some cultures, widows are burned up because they are considered no longer of any value.

Throughout generations women have experienced oppressions, abuses, and atrocities.

Prayer

"Your eternal Word, O Lord, stands firm in heaven. Your faithfulness extends to every generation, as enduring as the Earth You created." The population of the Earth has increased from 2 people to 6.8 billion, as have the number of sorrows. "Your laws remain true to this day, for everything serves

34

Your plans." "If Your laws hadn't sustained me with joy, I would have died in my misery. I will never forget Your commandments, for You have used them to restore my joy and my health." Father, in the name of Jesus, restore broken hearts filled with sorrow. We thank You for the atonement that You made for us; the price that You paid for us. We thank You for the "joy we find in Your presence;" for You give us "the oil of joy for mourning." We thank You because "You never forget about us. Our picture is indelibly tattooed in the palm of Your hand." "Nothing can separate us from Your love." "You provide for us." You "make a way for us in the wilderness." We give You praise. Amen.

(Ps. 119:89–93; Ps. 16:11; Isa. 61:3, 49:15–16; Rom. 8:39; Ps. 106:9)

"IN SORROW YOU SHALL BRING FORTH CHILDREN" (GEN. 3:16)

Infant mortality in the U.S. is 1 in 158 births. Thirty-eight million Americans live in poverty. Thirty-six percent of female heads of households live in poverty. Leah, Jacob's first wife, was very acquainted with sorrow. She gave her husband five sons, but nothing she did could win her husband's love.

Fatherless homes account for:

- 63 percent of youth suicides;

- 90 percent of homeless/runaway children;

- 85 percent of children with behavior problems;

- 71 percent of high school dropouts;

- 85 percent of youths in prison;

- Well over 50 percent of teen mothers.[19]

"TURN THE HEARTS OF THE FATHERS TO THE CHILDREN...LEST I COME AND STRIKE THE EARTH WITH A CURSE" (MAL. 4:6)

The United States is one of the wealthiest nations on the planet, unlike most of the world where billions of people live in small homes with dirt floors, no running water, and no electricity. Many nations do not have health insurance or health-care systems. If people are out of work, there is no unemployment support or welfare systems to provide any relief. Most places in the world do not have retirement pensions or social security benefits for the elderly. Many of the blessings that we take for granted, they do not have.

6,822,182,255	World population
-309,315,316	U.S. population
6,512,866,939	Most of the rest of the world lives in abject poverty

PRAYER

"The yoke was destroyed because of the anointing," and the curses are broken because of Jesus' shed blood. We declare "curses broken off" of families to become the kingdom You have ordained, in Jesus' name. Lord, we thank You that all fathers will become the righteous kings and priests of their families that You have ordained them to be; loving, protecting, and caring for their families; leading them in righteousness and praising Your name. Let the grief and the sorrow be remembered no more. "Repair the breach." Restore families in this nation and around the world in astounding

capacities that all will know that only You, God, could do this.

(Isa. 10:27; Gal. 3:13; Isa. 58:12)

Your desire shall be for your husband (Gen. 3:16)

Women are struggling because man cannot meet their needs and make them whole. In American culture, women are taught through cultural messages that a husband is needed to make them feel whole. In many other cultures, a husband is the only source of income, protection, and survival. No wonder so many women are trapped and confused by this lie of the devil.

The hunger and thirst of our souls is not for a man, but for God. Flesh can never completely satisfy. The human spirit desires and requires God. Without God breathing life into us, we are empty and dead. God is the Alpha and the Omega, the beginning and the end, the author and the finisher of our faith.

As the deer pants for streams of water, so my soul pants for you, O God.

—Psalm 42:1, niv

Prayer

Father, thank You for setting us free from the curses of the law. Thank You for making us free through the shed blood of Jesus Christ. We desire You, God. It is Your presence that we seek. As You said in Isaiah 54: "Fear not; you will no longer live in shame. Don't be afraid; there is no more disgrace for you. You will no longer remember the shame of your youth and the sorrows of widowhood. For your Creator will be your husband; the Lord of Heaven's Armies is his name! He is your Redeemer, the Holy One of Israel, the God of all the earth. For the Lord has called you back from your grief—as though you were a young wife abandoned by her husband," says your God. "For a brief moment I abandoned you, but with great compassion I will take you back. In a burst of anger I turned my face away for a little while. But with everlasting love I will have compassion on you," says the Lord, your Redeemer. "Just as I swore in the time of Noah that I would never again let a flood cover the earth, so now I swear that I will never again be angry and punish you. For the mountains may move and the hills disappear, but even then my faithful love for you will remain. My covenant of blessing will never be broken," says the Lord, who has mercy on you. We thank You for these blessings, in Jesus' name. Amen.

It's a Girl!

"It's a girl!" the doctor, nurse, or midwife proudly announces. The birth of a child should be a time of joy in any home. Children are a blessing from the Lord. Sadly, in some countries that announcement is a death warrant. In many others, it means a new servant or slave has been added. Even still in America today, that beautiful child is often thought of and treated as less than another. The disappointment that it wasn't a boy may not show through in the countenance and outward expression on the father's face, but it is undeniably transmitted in the spirit from the father to the mother, then through the mother to the child. A wound of rejection has been inflicted on that child's spirit in the very essence of her being. This wounding is continued throughout life through various social customs, practices, and stigmas around the world and in the U.S. For many women this is the root. For most it is the beginning, the genesis of feelings of inferiority, lack of self-confidence, esteem, and worth. These feelings or ways of thinking about oneself keep many women from rising into their rightful positions in co-dominion.

Consider the following statistics:[20]

- One United Nations estimate says from 113 million to 200 million women around the world are demographically "missing." Every year, from 1.5 million to 3 million women and girls lose their lives as a result of gender-based violence or neglect.

- In countries where the birth of a boy is considered a gift and the birth of a girl a curse from the gods, selective abortion and infanticide eliminate female babies.

- Young girls die disproportionately from neglect because food and medical attention are given first to brothers, fathers, husbands, and sons.

- In countries where women are considered the property of men, their fathers and brothers can murder them for choosing their own sexual partners. These are called "honor" killings, though honor has nothing to do with it.

- Young brides are killed if their fathers do not pay sufficient money to the men who have married them. These are called "dowry deaths," although they are not just deaths, they are murders.

God's desire for men and women is to have co-dominion in the earth, working together with God to rule His kingdom in holiness and righteousness. When there is agreement between a husband and a wife there is no power on earth that can stop them. There is peace in the home, children come into alignment, and finances come into order. More importantly, when the two come into agreement in prayer, the power of their prayer and the impact that it has on the earth is multiplied exponentially. "One can chase a thousand, two can chase ten thousand" (Deut. 32:30). No demons can stand against two in agreement. In prayer together, we can change the horrible devastations we see taking place in the earth. When men and women come together in unity, the Holy Spirit moves powerfully to change individuals and to change the world, just as He did on the Day of Pentecost. In this hour of church restoration, this Esther generation is called as God's secret weapon to fulfill His plans. Women have unique feminine ability, grace, skill, and wisdom. Women are the ones that bring life into the world, nurture the young, and hold families together. Women have the grace and wisdom to bring people together. The whole earth is waiting for us to come into alignment with God's plan. We are equal partners in God's gift of new life! When the full army of God comes together, comprised of women and men in co-dominion in the kingdom, we will be able to take back all that the enemy has stolen from us. When we stand in unity there is tremendous blessing! "For there the Lord commanded the blessing—Life forevermore" (Ps. 133). When the body of Christ fulfills Ephesians 5:22–33 with the husband and the wife coming together as one, Christ will return for His bride without spot or wrinkle!

Prayer

O you afflicted one, Tossed with tempest, and not comforted, Behold, I will lay your stones with colorful gems, And lay your foundations with sapphires. I will make your pinnacles of rubies, Your gates of crystal, And all your walls of precious stones. All your children shall be taught by the Lord, And great shall be the peace of your children. In righteousness you shall be established; You shall be far from oppression, for you shall not fear; And from terror, for it shall not come near you....No weapon formed against you shall prosper, And every tongue which rises against you in judgment You shall condemn. This is the heritage of the servants of the Lord, And their righteousness is from Me," Says the Lord.
　　　　　　　　　　　　　*—*Isaiah 54:11–14, 17

Thank You, Father, for these great and precious promises. We stand on Your Word and declare it true in our lives. For You execute righteous judgment for all that are oppressed. Father, thank You for raising us up to sit in heavenly places in Christ Jesus. You have caused us to be above and not beneath, the head and not the tail. Thank You, God, for Jesus Christ who has set us free. Not only have You set us free, You have also put us in a place of heavenly authority to reign and rule with You. So, now we take our rightful place of co-dominion in the Earth. Thy will be done on Earth as it is in heaven. We pray this prayer in Jesus' name. Amen.

CONCLUSION

And so, Father, as we pray these prayers, we commend them to You. Your Word does not return void. We thank You for transforming Your church into a bride without spot or wrinkle that will take dominion in the Earth. We thank You for bringing deliverance, salvation, and transformation to hurting women all over the world, in Jesus' name. We thank You for bringing joy and peace to all men as they love and cherish their wives. We thank

You that both men and women will take their rightful places in the kingdom—the husband and the wife walking in biblical knowledge of created purpose, walking in co-dominion in the Earth as the Word clearly declares. We look for Your soon return for Your prepared bride. We pray these prayers in Jesus' name. Amen.

As stated at the beginning of this book, the purpose of this ministry is to provide prayer support for women, children, and families all over the world. Please continue to pray with me and encourage others to join in our efforts as we war in the Spirit to bring deliverance to women, and restoration and transformation to the body of Christ. A portion of the profits from this book will be used to support ministries that bring deliverance and support to women and children in many places in the world.

As I worked with and prayed for children in schools, I saw them transformed from failures into scholars, no longer bound by circumstances such as poverty, abuse, addictions, and broken homes that once held them captive.

God is able to transform you into the image of Christ:

- He is able to heal the broken places in your life.

- He is able to raise you up to sit in heavenly places.

- He has already provided the victory for you. All you have to do is receive it by faith.

If you would like to receive Christ into your heart, pray this prayer with me.

Jesus, right now I confess Your lordship over my life, and I believe in my heart that God the Father raised You from the dead to save me a sinner. I accept Your work of salvation and grace for my life and my heart. I am sorry and repent of my sin. I now declare your Lordship over my life. Thank You for saving me. Amen.

About the Author

Rev. Thelma C. Smith has served in the public educational system as a secondary school administrator and high school science teacher for over twenty-three years, helping young people fulfill their destinies and maximize their potential. She has served in ministry for the past thirty years delivering a powerful message of hope through salvation in Jesus Christ.

She has published "After God's Heart," a web page to provide online prayer support for women, children, and families all over the world. It will focus prayer in spiritual realms to bring deliverance to women, and restoration and transformation to the body of Christ.

Thelma resides in Virginia Beach, Virginia, with her husband, Pierce. They have three adult children.

TO CONTACT THE AUTHOR

If you need prayer or would like to share your testimony, we would love to hear from you. Donations and gifts to this ministry are welcome. Please contact us at:

AGHministries@yahoo.com

ℐotes

Chapter 3
Prayer Targets

1. Isabella L. Horon and Diana Cheng, "Enhanced Surveillance for Pregnancy-Associated Mortality— Maryland 1993–1998," *Journal of the American Medical Association* 285, no. 11 (2001): 1455–1459.

2. Patricia Tjaden and Nancy Thoennes, "Extent, Nature and Consequences of Intimate Partner Violence: Findings from the National Violence Against Women Survey" (Washington, DC: National Insitute of Justice and the Centers of Disease Control and Prevention, 2000); Sara Glazer, "Violence Against Women," *Congressional Quarterly* 3, no. 8 (1993): 171; The Commonwealth Fund, "Health Concerns Across a Woman's Lifespan," *Survey of Women's Health*, 1999; www.clarkprosecutor.org/html/domviol/facts.htm (accessed June 18, 2010).

3. Callie Marie Rennison, "Crime Data Brief: Intimate Partner Violence, 1993–2001," Bureau of Justice Statistics, 2003, available at http://www.ojp.usdoj.gov/bjs/pub/pdf/ipv01.pdf (accessed June 18, 2010).

4. FBI Uniform Crime Report Expanded Homicide Database 2, "Murder Victims by Age, Sex, Race," 2008, available at www.fbi.gov/ucr/cius2008/offenses/expanded_information/data/shrtable_02.html (accessed

June 18, 2010).

5. "Women and Violence," Hearings before the U.S. Senate Judiciary Committee, August 29 and December 11, 1990, Senate Hearing 101-939, p. 12, available at http://www.bucoks.com/depts/attorney/domestic.htm (accessed June 18, 2010).

6. Jill Smolowe, Ann Blackman, Wendy Cole, Scott Norvell, Elizabeth Rudulph, Andrea Sachs, and Richard Woodbury, "When Violence Hits Home," *Time,* July 4, 1994, available at http://www.time.com/time/magazine/article/0,9171,981054,00.html (accessed June 18, 2010).

7. S.R. Martin, S. Holsapfels, and P. Baker, "Wife Abuse: Are We Detecting It?" *Journal of Women's Health*, 1992, 77–80; Evan Stark and Anne Flitcraft, U.S. Senate Committee on the Judiciary, Hearings on Women and Violence, August 29 and December 11, 1990; "Ten Facts About Violence Against Women" available at http://www.sedgwickcounty.org/da/dv_facts.html (accessed June 18, 2010).

8. Ibid.

9. Information available online at en.wikipedia.org/wiki/Women_in_Islam (accessed June 18, 2010).

10. Jennifer Baker, "The Accuracy of Divorce Statistics," http://lawprofessors.typepad.com/family_law/2010/05/the-accuracy-of-divorce-statistics.html (accessed June 22,2101).

11. National Marriage Project, "The State of Our Unions," Rutgers University, 2005, available at http://www.terryreal.com/press/pdfs/marriage_divorce_in_

america-FS.pdf (accessed June 18, 2010).

12. Ibid.

13. Lale Say, Mie Inoue, Samuel Mills, and Emi Suzuki, "Maternal Mortality in 2005: Estimates Developed by WHO, UNICEF, UNFPA, and The World Bank," World Health Organization, 2007, p. 16, available at www.who.int.whosis/mme_2005.pdf (accessed June 21, 2010).

14. Abortion facts available at http://www.abortionno.org/Resources/fastfacts.html (accessed June 21, 2010).

15. Information available online at www.PolarisProject.org/content/view/26/47 (accessed June 21, 2010).

16. Ibid.

17. Information available online at http://en.wikipedia.org/wiki/Religion_in_the_United_States and http://www.thearda.com/mapsReports/reports/US_2000.asp (accessed June 18, 2010).

18. "Most Christian Nations" available at http://www.TheArda.com/QuickLists/QuickList_42.asp (accessed June 21, 2010).

19. Statistics available online at www.divorcemag.com/statistics/statsUS2002.shtml (accessed June 18, 2010).

20. Ayaan Hirsi Ali, "Women Go 'Missing' by the Millions," http://www.nytimes.com/2006/03/24/opinion/24iht-edali.html (accessed June 22, 2010).